EID AL-FITR

KATHRYN WALTON

PowerKiDS press™

T0395670

Published in 2026 by The Rosen Publishing Group, Inc.
2544 Clinton Street, Buffalo, NY 14224

First Edition

Editor: Greg Roza
Book Design: Rachel Rising

Photo Credits: Cover, p. 1 Fevziie/Shutterstock.com; pp. 4, 6, 8, 10, 12, 14, 16, 18, 20 Vjom/Shutterstock.com; p. 5 szefei/Shutterstock.com; p. 7 YusufAslan/Shutterstock.com; p. 9 Lens Hitam/Shutterstock.com; p. 11 TabitaZn/Shutterstock.com; p. 13 Odua Images/Shutterstock.com; p. 15 Rujman/Shutterstock.com; p. 17 Odua Images/Shutterstock.com; p. 19 Tompel/Shutterstock.com; p. 21 https://commons.wikimedia.org/wiki/File:Obama_hosts_Iftar_dinner_on_Ramadan.jpg.

Some of the images in this book illustrate individuals who are models. The depictions do not imply actual situations or events.

Cataloging-in-Publication Data

Names: Walton, Kathryn, 1993-.
Title: Eid al-Fitr / Kathryn Walton.
Description: Buffalo, New York : PowerKids Press, 2026. | Series: World celebrations | Includes glossary and index.
Identifiers: ISBN 9781499452129 (pbk.) | ISBN 9781499452136 (library bound) | ISBN 9781499452143 (ebook)
Subjects: LCSH: Eid al-Fitr–Juvenile literature. | Ramadan–Juvenile literature. | Fasts and feasts–Islam–Juvenile literature.
Classification: LCC BP186.4 W367 2026 | DDC 297.3'8–dc23

Manufactured in the United States of America

CPSIA Compliance Information: Batch #CSPK26. For Further Information contact Rosen Publishing at 1-800-237-9932.

Find us on

CONTENTS

The End of Ramadan

Islam is one of the largest religions in the world. People who follow Islam are called Muslims. They pray to the God Allah. Muslims are expected to strengthen their belief in Allah during the Muslim month of Ramadan. The last day of Ramadan is Eid al-Fitr.

What Is Ramadan?

Ramadan is the ninth month of the Muslim calendar. It is a month of prayer, deep thinking, and kindness to others. Muslims fast during Ramadan. This means they can't eat food between sunup and sundown for the whole month. The purpose of fasting is to teach Muslims **self-restraint.**

Breaking the Fast

Eid al-Fitr means "**Festival** of Breaking Fast." It is a chance for Muslims to thank Allah for giving them the strength to fast during Ramadan. It is a day of joy, togetherness, and peace. The day begins with group prayers. Then Muslims celebrate with festivals and foods!

Hanging Lanterns

Muslims clean and **decorate** their homes in the days leading up to Eid al-Fitr. Lanterns, or lamps, called fanous are hung in and around homes. They are hung in the community too. They stand for light overcoming dark. Children make colorful paper lanterns.

Eid Mubarak!

Eid al-Fitr is a time to honor family. People wear their best clothes! Adults give gifts and money to kids. Kids give gifts to each other and their grandparents. Muslims may call family members to wish them "Eid Mubarak!" That means "blessed festival!"

Gathering to Eat

Food is a fun part of Eid al-Fitr. Candies, cookies, and other sweets are common. Fruits called dates are often served before the meal. The main meal is often slow-cooked dishes with meats and vegetables. In India, many families eat biryani, a dish made with rice, meat, and **spices**.

What Is Zakat?

Zakat is a Muslim belief that means "giving to the poor." Zakat al-Fitr is a special part of Eid al-Fitr. Muslims must give food or money to the needy at the end of Ramadan. This allows poor people to celebrate Eid al-Fitr too.

Around the World

Eid al-Fitr is celebrated differently in some countries. Many countries have **fireworks**! Some Muslims decorate their hands with an art called henna. Muslims eat different food depending on the country too. In Indonesia, Muslims make ketupat. This is made of rice inside coconut leaves.

In the White House!

The Muslim holiday of Eid al-Fitr was first celebrated in the White House in 1805! President Thomas Jefferson held a dinner for an official from the African country of Tunisia. The White House has held an Eid al-Fitr dinner most years since 1996.

GLOSSARY

decorate: To make something interesting or beautiful by adding things to it.

festival: A time of celebration in honor of something or someone special.

fireworks: A display of explosions and light high in the air created by the burning of chemicals.

self-restraint: The ability to stop yourself from doing something.

spice: Something that makes food taste better or different.

FOR MORE INFORMATION

BOOKS

Ferguson, Melissa. *Ramadan and Eid al-Fitr*. Mankato, MN: Capstone, 2021.

Kazi, Natashia Kahn. *Moon's Ramadan*. Boston, MA: Houghton Mifflin Harcourt, 2023.

WEBSITES

Eid al-Fitr Facts for Kids
kids.kiddle.co/Eid_al-Fitr
Read more about Eid al-Fitr here.

10 Amazing Facts Ramadan Facts for Kids
nooracademy.com/10-amazing-ramadan-facts-for-kids
You can learn more about the month of Ramadan and what it means to Muslims at this website.

INDEX